ROSE ELLIOT

Cheese Dishes

ROSE ELLIOT

Cheese Dishes

Photography by Simon Wheeler

WEIDENFELD & NICOLSON

Rose Elliot

Rose Elliot is Britain's foremost vegetarian cookery writer; she has played a key role in transforming the image and taste of vegetarian food. She has written more than 45 books, making her one of the bestselling vegetarian cookery writers in the English-speaking world. Her books include *Not Just a Load of Old Lentils*, which has been continuously in print since it was published in 1972 and *The Bean Book*, described as 'as essential to a student as a dictionary and a thesaurus'; and more recently *The Classic Vegetarian Cookbook* and *Vegetarian Cookery* (published in a new edition in 1996).

Though a life-long vegetarian, Rose's main concern is not to convert meat-eaters, but simply to share the delicious flavours of vegetarian food. Her cookery demonstrations are in great demand, and she writes for a variety of newspapers and magazines.

Contents

THE BASICS

Strange to see how
a good dinner and feasting
reconciles everyone.

SAMUEL PEPYS

Introduction

Cheese is one of the most versatile, nourishing and convenient ingredients. It can be served hot, cold, cooked or uncooked; as a starter, in soups, in snacks and salads, as a main course and even as a pudding. I have aimed to reflect this versatility in the recipes I have chosen for this book; the recipes also use a variety of different types of cheese.

When I started writing about vegetarian cookery it was impossible to buy cheese made without animal rennet; now, a sign of the times perhaps, there are many. If you're not sure, ask in the shop, because some cheeses which are vegetarian do not advertise the fact. I hope that you will enjoy trying different cheeses as you make the dishes in this book.

You will find that these dishes are all quite quick and easy to make, because that's another advantage of cheese: you can get an excellent result without too much time and effort. Just remember to keep the rest of the meal relatively low in fat to offset the richness of the cheese and you will end up with a delightful and well-balanced meal.

Ros Hurst

Deep-fried camembert
with apricot sauce

SERVES 4

2 whole Camembert (250 g/9 oz
  each), not too ripe
2 eggs, beaten
125 g/4 oz dried breadcrumbs
225 g/8 oz apricot jam
juice of ½ lemon
vegetable oil for deep-frying
salad leaves for serving

If the Camembert is not the kind which has already
been cut into sections, cut each cheese into six equal
portions. Put the beaten eggs into a bowl, and the
breadcrumbs in another. Dip the pieces of Camembert
into the egg, then into the crumbs, to coat them evenly.
Repeat the process so that they are really well coated.
Chill them in the refrigerator for at least 30 minutes.

Put the apricot jam into a saucepan with the lemon
juice and melt it over a very gentle heat.

To serve, heat the oil for deep-frying. To test that it
is at the right temperature, dip the end of a wooden
chopstick or wooden spoon into it: the oil should
bubble immediately. Carefully lower some of the pieces
of Camembert into the hot oil and fry for 4–5 minutes,
until they are crisp and golden brown. Remove them
with a slotted spoon and drain on crumpled kitchen
paper. Keep them warm while you fry the rest,
then serve immediately, with the apricot sauce and
a salad garnish.

*Serve as a first course before a vegetable or grain-based meal
(such as risotto), or as a meal in itself, accompanied with a leafy
green salad with a light dressing. Finish the meal with a
refreshing pudding, for example a compote of fruits of the forest:
strawberries, raspberries, redcurrants and blueberries.*

Roquefort, pear and walnut salad with watercress

SERVES 4

2 sweet ripe pears such as
  Comice
juice of ½ lemon
85 g/3 oz washed and prepared
  watercress
200 g/7 oz Roquefort cheese
12 walnuts, cracked and shells
  removed

Peel, quarter and core the pears, then cut them into long thin slices and sprinkle with the lemon juice. Arrange the slices of pear on a serving platter or on four individual plates, together with the watercress. Slice the cheese or break it into pieces and add to the plates, along with the walnuts. Serve at once.

Alternatively, you can put all the ingredients into a salad bowl – a glass one is nice – and toss them together lightly.

Serve as a first course before a meal of grilled fish or, for vegetarians, puréed white beans with grilled red and yellow peppers, new potatoes and green salad.

Stilton and celery soup

SERVES 4

1 head of celery, tough outer
  stems removed
15 g/½ oz butter
1 onion, chopped
900 ml/1½ pints vegetable
  stock
1 teaspoon cornflour
150 ml/5 fl oz single cream
125 g/4 oz Stilton cheese,
  crumbled
salt and pepper

Wash and chop the celery. Heat the butter in a large saucepan and add the onion; cover and cook gently for 5 minutes, then add the celery. Stir, then cover and cook gently for a further 10 minutes or so – don't let the vegetables brown.

Pour in the stock, then cover the pan and leave to simmer over a low heat for 30–40 minutes, or until the celery is very tender.

Purée half the mixture in a liquidizer or food processor, then return it to the saucepan. Mix the cornflour with the cream until smooth and add to the pan, together with the Stilton. Stir over a low heat until the soup has thickened slightly and the cheese has melted – don't let it boil. Season to taste and serve at once

Serve with warm rolls as a first course to a festive meal: turkey for meat-eaters or mixed mushrooms with wild rice for vegetarians, accompanied by piquant Brussels sprouts with lime zest and juice.

Young spinach salad with red onions and parmesan

SERVES 4

3 tablespoons olive oil
1 tablespoon red wine vinegar
1 garlic clove, crushed
salt and pepper
1 red or purple onion, thinly
  sliced
225 g/8 oz tender young spinach
  leaves
125 g/4 oz Parmesan cheese

Put the olive oil, vinegar, garlic and some salt and pepper into a salad bowl and mix to make a dressing. Add the onion rings and stir so that they are all coated with the dressing, then set aside until just before you want to serve the salad. This can be done an hour or so in advance if you wish, to give the onion a chance to soften and mellow in the dressing.

Meanwhile wash the spinach leaves thoroughly and leave in a colander to drain. Make shavings of Parmesan using a potato peeler or a sharp knife.

Just before you want to serve the salad, add the spinach to the bowl and toss in the dressing; taste and adjust the seasoning, then add the Parmesan and toss lightly. Serve at once.

Serve as a light meal with an interesting bread such as walnut. Finish with ripe peaches or nectarines, served as they are, or sliced and marinated with a little sugar and white wine.

TWICE-BAKED GRUYÈRE SOUFFLÉS

3 ramekins ! [handwritten]

SERVES 4

1½ oz [handwritten]

8 tablespoons dry grated
  Parmesan cheese
225 g/8 oz skimmed milk soft
  cheese
4 eggs, separated, plus 1 egg
  white
150 g/5 oz Gruyère cheese,
  grated
salt and pepper

Preheat the oven to 180°C/350°F/Gas Mark 4.
Generously grease 8 ramekins or tea cups, then sprinkle
the insides with 4 tablespoons of the Parmesan.

Put the soft cheese into a bowl and mash it until
smooth, then gradually mix in the egg yolks and half
the grated Gruyère cheese. Using a clean, grease-free
whisk, whisk the egg whites until they form firm peaks.
Stir a heaped tablespoon of the beaten whites into the
egg yolk mixture to loosen it, then gently fold in the
rest of the egg whites.

Spoon the mixture into the ramekins or cups: it can
come level with the top, but don't pile it up any higher.
Stand them in a roasting tin, pour boiling water around
them so that it comes halfway up the sides of the
ramekins, then bake for 15 minutes, until the soufflés
are risen and set.

Remove them from the oven and leave them to cool;
they'll sink a bit. Then loosen the edges and turn them
out; it's easiest to turn them out on to your hand.
Transfer them to an ovenproof serving dish. Sprinkle
each one first with the remaining Gruyère cheese, then
with the rest of the Parmesan. They can now wait until
you are ready to bake them.

To serve, preheat the oven to 220°C/425°F/Gas
Mark 7. Bake the soufflés for 15-20 minutes, until they
are puffed up and golden brown. Serve at once.

*Serve these as a starter before a simple salad meal.
Alternatively, for a main course, serve them with a fresh tomato
sauce or tomato and basil salad and steamed green beans;
follow with fresh fruit salad and thick yogurt.*

FRIED HALLOUMI
with a piquant dressing

SERVES 4

grated rind and juice of ½ lemon
1 tablespoon red wine vinegar
1 teaspoon Dijon mustard
1 garlic clove, crushed
3 tablespoons olive oil, plus
    extra for shallow-frying
2 tablespoons fresh flat-leaf
    parsley, chopped
1–2 tablespoons capers, rinsed
    and drained
salt and pepper
225 g/8 oz halloumi cheese
salad leaves for serving

First make the dressing. Put the lemon rind and juice into a small bowl with the vinegar, mustard, garlic and 3 tablespoons of olive oil and whisk together until they emulsify. Add the parsley, 1 or 2 tablespoons of capers, according to your taste, and some salt and pepper. Set aside.

Drain any water from the halloumi, then rinse the cheese under the tap to remove any excess saltiness; pat dry on kitchen paper. Cut the halloumi into slices, 7 mm/⅓ inch thick.

Heat a little olive oil in a frying pan, then fry the halloumi until golden brown – it browns quickly, so you will probably find that by the time you've put the last slice in, the first one will need turning over. When the slices are browned on both sides, take them out and drain them on kitchen paper. Serve immediately, with the dressing and some salad leaves.

Serve as a vegetarian main course with a leafy green salad or a simple tomato salad, or with steamed young vegetables. Finish the meal with a yogurt-based fruit fool, or pears poached in red wine and ginger.

GOATS CHEESE EN CROÛTE
with cranberry sauce

SERVES 4

450 g/1 lb ready-rolled
  puff pastry
2 x 100 g/3½ oz goats' cheese
  logs
a little beaten egg or milk, to
  glaze

Cranberry sauce
175 g/6 oz cranberries
85 g/3 oz sugar
1 tablespoon port or fresh
  orange juice

Preheat the oven to 220°C/425°F/Gas Mark 7. Roll out the pastry thinly and cut out eight circles which are 2.5 cm/1 inch bigger in diameter than the goats' cheese. Cut the cheeses in half horizontally.

Place one halved goats' cheese on one of the pastry circles, cut side up – this will prevent it from oozing out during cooking. Brush the edge of the pastry lightly with cold water, put another pastry circle on top and press the edges firmly together or crimp with a fork. Repeat with the rest of the cheese and pastry.

Prick the tops to allow the steam to escape, and brush the tops lightly with beaten egg or milk. Decorate with pastry trimmings and brush again with egg or milk, then place on a baking sheet which has been brushed with water and bake for 15 minutes.

While the cheeses are cooking, make the sauce. Put the cranberries into a saucepan with 4 tablespoons water. Bring to the boil, then simmer for about 10 minutes, until the berries are tender. Add the sugar and simmer gently until it has dissolved. Remove from the heat and add the port or fresh orange juice. Serve warm with the freshly baked goats' cheeses en croûte.

These make a lovely vegetarian Christmas dish, especially if you decorate them with pastry holly leaves and berries. Serve with stir-fried Brussels sprouts, steamed carrots and creamy mashed potatoes; start with something simple and fruity such as sliced pears and watercress, and finish with lemon or champagne sorbet.

FETA FRITTATA WITH SUN-DRIED TOMATOES

SERVES 4

4 eggs
salt and pepper
1 tablespoon olive oil
200 g/7 oz feta cheese, drained
    and cubed
6 sun-dried tomatoes, chopped
sprigs of flat-leaf parsley, torn

Preheat the grill. Beat the eggs with 1 tablespoon of cold water, with salt and pepper to taste.

Heat the olive oil in a frying pan – a 20 cm/8 inch one is ideal – then pour in the beaten eggs. Put the feta cheese on top of the egg mixture, then the sun-dried tomatoes, distributing them evenly. Leave to cook, undisturbed, for 3–4 minutes, until the bottom is golden brown and the top is beginning to set.

Put the frying pan under the hot grill for a further 2–3 minutes to cook the top of the frittata. Serve at once, in thick wedges, scattered with the flat-leaf parsley. It's also very good cold.

Serve with a green salad – rocket or Cos lettuce continue the Mediterranean theme. Finish with strawberries, peaches or nectarines, or whatever fresh fruit is in season.

AUBERGINE, MOZZARELLA AND TOMATO LAYER

SERVES 2

3 tablespoons olive oil
1 onion, chopped
1 garlic clove, crushed
1 x 425 g/15 oz can tomatoes
salt and pepper
1 aubergine
125 g/4 oz mozzarella cheese
25 g/1 oz Parmesan cheese,
   grated

Heat 1 tablespoon of the olive oil in a saucepan, add the onion and garlic, cover and cook gently for 10 minutes.

Add the tomatoes, breaking them up with a spoon, then leave to simmer, uncovered, for about 20 minutes, until the sauce is very thick. Season to taste.

Preheat the grill and set the oven to 200°C/400°F/Gas Mark 6. Remove the stem from the aubergine, then cut the aubergine horizontally three times to make four slices. Brush the slices with the remaining oil, then put them under the hot grill until they are lightly browned on both sides. Cut the mozzarella cheese into thin slices.

On a baking sheet, reassemble the aubergine, sandwiching each layer with tomato sauce, grated Parmesan cheese and slices of mozzarella. Press it together gently but firmly, then bake in the oven for 20 minutes, or until the cheese has melted. Some liquid will probably ooze out from the sauce but this doesn't matter; and if the aubergine lurches a bit to one side, just gently push it together again. Cut in half to serve.

Serve as a vegetarian main course with cooked green beans and a leafy salad, perhaps including some fresh basil. Start the meal with carrot and coriander soup, and finish with fresh dates and yogurt.

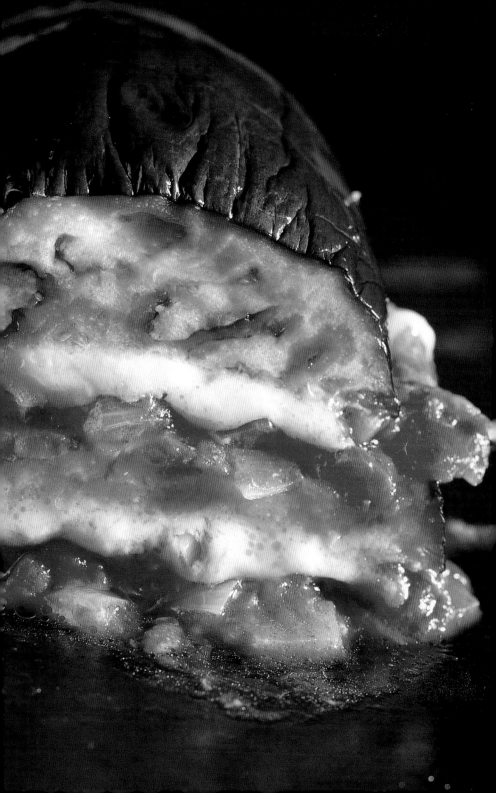

CHEDDAR CHEESE BISCUITS

MAKES 20

85 g/3 oz plain wholewheat flour
pinch of cayenne pepper
50 g/2 oz butter, at room
   temperature
50 g/2 oz strongly flavoured
   Cheddar cheese, grated

Preheat the oven to 200°C/400°F/Gas Mark 6.

Sift the flour and cayenne pepper into a bowl, adding any residue of bran left in the sieve. Add the butter to the bowl, then use a fork to mix it thoroughly with the flour. Mix in the grated cheese to make a dough.

Roll the dough into a sausage shape, then, using a sharp knife, cut off slices about 5 mm/¼ inch thick and place these on a baking sheet, pressing them gently into shape if necessary. Leave a little space between them, but they won't spread much. Bake for about 10 minutes, or until the biscuits are golden brown.

Leave on the baking sheet to cool slightly, then transfer to a wire rack to become completely cold and crisp.

If you make small biscuits, they are good nibbles to have with drinks. They could also be served as an accompaniment to a soup such as watercress. Alternatively, for a light lunch, offer them with a cheese board, nuts and celery, perhaps followed by little coffee custards.

Raisin and curd cheese tart

SERVES 6–8

225 g/8 oz shortcrust pastry
(page 35)
225 g/8 oz curd cheese or low-
fat soft cheese
125 g/4 oz caster sugar
150 ml/5 fl oz double cream
3 eggs, beaten
50 g/2 oz raisins

Preheat the oven to 190°C/375°F/Gas Mark 5. Roll out the pastry and use to line a 22 cm/9 inch flan dish; ease the pastry into the dish, press it down and trim off any excess. Prick the base lightly with a fork, then put a circle of greaseproof paper on top of the pastry and weigh it down with baking beans or pastry trimmings. Bake for 10–15 minutes, then remove the paper and beans or pastry trimmings and bake for a further 5–10 minutes, until the pastry is crisp.

Leave the pastry to cool slightly while you make the filling. Beat together the cheese, sugar, cream and eggs, until smooth. Scatter the raisins evenly over the pastry base, then pour the cheese mixture on top. Put the tart into the oven, turn the temperature down to 160°C/325°F/Gas Mark 3 and bake for 30–35 minutes, until set. Leave to cool. Serve the tart at room temperature or chilled, with some pouring cream or crème fraîche.

Serve after a main course that includes plenty of colourful vegetables; perhaps spinach lasagne with steamed carrots. This tart also makes a delicious mid-morning or afternoon treat with a cup of tea or coffee.

MASCARPONE AND LEMON ICE CREAM

SERVES 6

grated zest and juice of 2 lemons
125 g/4 oz caster sugar
4 large egg yolks
500 g/1 lb 2 oz mascarpone
   cheese

Make the lemon juice up to 150 ml/5 fl oz with water, then put into a saucepan with the lemon zest and sugar. Heat gently until the sugar has dissolved, then boil until syrupy – about 4 minutes.

Meanwhile, in a large heatproof bowl, whisk the egg yolks until they are quite thick and pale. Whisking continuously, strain the hot syrup over the egg yolks. Set the bowl over a pan of simmering water and whisk for a further 5 minutes or so, until very thick and pale. Leave to cool slightly, then whisk in the mascarpone cheese.

Pour the mixture into a plastic container and freeze until firm; or use an ice cream maker. Remove from the freezer for 15 minutes or so before serving, to allow the ice cream to soften a little.

Serve on its own or with fresh fruit such as raspberries to finish off a special summer meal; perhaps a mixed rice pilaf with fresh asparagus and summer vegetables and a garden herb salad.

The Basics

VEGETABLE STOCK

MAKES ABOUT 1 LITRE/1¾ PINTS

1 kg/2½ lb mixed vegetables and
trimmings, such as onions,
carrot trimmings, celery, leek
trimmings, parsley stalks
several garlic cloves, unpeeled
2 bay leaves
1 tablespoon black peppercorns
1 or 2 sprigs of thyme
strip of lemon peel (optional)

Put all the ingredients into a large saucepan and cover
with about 1.3 litres/2¼ pints water. Bring to the boil,
then cover and leave to simmer for 30–40 minutes until
the vegetables are very soft. Leave to cool.

Strain through a sieve and keep in a covered container
in the refrigerator. Use within four days. Alternatively,
freeze in small quantities and use as required.

An easy way to ensure a supply of stock is to make
a habit of saving the water strained from cooking
vegetables; if you do this you also conserve the nutrients
which would otherwise be lost in the cooking water.

Shortcrust pastry

MAKES ENOUGH TO LINE A 22 CM/
9 INCH FLAN TIN

85 g/3 oz plain flour
85 g/3 oz wholewheat flour
85 g/3 oz butter, chilled and diced

Sifting the flours together into a bowl or food processor, adding the residue of bran left in the sieve. Add the butter, then whizz the mixture in the food processor or rub the butter in with your fingertips until the mixture resembles breadcrumbs. Add 6 teaspoons of ice-cold water and mix briefly until the mixture comes together to make a dough. If possible, chill for 20–30 minutes before rolling out.

Techniques

BAKING BLIND

Pastry cases often need to be baked blind. Sometimes this is to help the pastry to remain crisp, sometimes it is because the filling is cooked at a lower temperature or for a shorter time than it would take to cook the pastry.

To bake a pastry case blind, preheat the oven to 200°C/ 400°F/Gas Mark 6. Roll out the pastry and ease into the tin, pressing gently against the sides, then trim away any excess pastry. Prick the base of the pastry lightly all over with a fork. Line the pastry with a piece of non-stick baking paper and weigh it down with dried beans, special baking beans, old crusts or some of the pastry trimmings. Bake in the preheated oven for 15 minutes, then remove the paper and beans or trimmings and return the pastry to the oven for a further 5 minutes, or until the base is set and beginning to turn golden.

SHAPING BISCUITS

An easy way to shape biscuits made from a fairly firm dough is to form the dough into a sausage shape and then cut off slices about 5 mm/1/4 inch thick. You can keep the roll round, or flatten it a bit to make biscuits which are more oval or rectangular in shape. If you make extra dough and keep a roll of it, well-wrapped, in the freezer, you will be able to cut off a few biscuits and bake them fresh when you need them. This is what the Americans call 'ice-box cookies'.

DEEP-FRYING

Use a deep, heavy pan: it should be deep enough that by the time the food has been put in the oil will not come further than halfway up the pan. It should also be sturdy and heavy enough to withstand high temperatures without warping.

Successful deep-frying means that the food is sealed the instant it meets the hot fat. To test whether the oil is hot enough, drop in a small cube of bread: it should immediately sizzle and rise to the surface of the oil. Alternatively, dip a wooden chopstick or the end of a wooden spoon into the oil: if it is hot enough, bubbles will form immediately.

Food to be deep-fried should be as dry as possible before putting it into the hot oil, to avoid spluttering.

After deep-frying, use a slotted spoon or fat drainer to lift out the food and transfer it to crumpled kitchen paper to drain.

Classic Cooking

Starters
Jean Christophe Novelli Chef/patron of Maison Novelli, which opened in London to great acclaim in 1996. He previously worked at the Four Seasons restaurant, London.

Vegetable Soups
Elisabeth Luard Cookery writer for the *Sunday Telegraph Magazine* and author of *European Peasant Food* and *European Festival Food*, which won a Glenfiddich Award.

Gourmet Salads
Sonia Stevenson The first woman chef in the UK to be awarded a Michelin star, at the Horn of Plenty in Devon. Author of *The Magic of Saucery* and *Fresh Ways with Fish*.

Fish and Shellfish
Gordon Ramsay Chef/proprietor of one of London's most popular restaurants, Aubergine, recently awarded its second Michelin star. He is the author of *A Passion for Flavour*.

Chicken, Duck and Game
Nick Nairn Chef/patron of Braeval restaurant near Aberfoyle in Scotland, whose BBC-TV series *Wild Harvest* was last summer's most successful cookery series, accompanied by a book.

Livers, Sweetbreads and Kidneys
Simon Hopkinson Former chef/patron at London's Bibendum restaurant, columnist and author of *Roast Chicken and Other Stories* and the forthcoming *The Prawn Cocktail Years*.

Vegetarian
Rosamond Richardson Author of several vegetarian titles, including *The Great Green Gourmet* and *Food from Green Places*. She has also appeared on television.

Pasta
Joy Davies One of the creators of *BBC Good Food Magazine*, she has been food editor of *She, Woman* and *Options* and written for the *Guardian, Daily Telegraph* and *Harpers & Queen*.

Cheese Dishes
Rose Elliot The UK's most successful vegetarian cookery writer and author of many books, including *Not Just a Load of Old Lentils* and *The Classic Vegetarian Cookbook*.

Potato Dishes
Patrick McDonald Author of the forthcoming *Simply Good Food* and Harvey Nichols' food consultant.

Bistro Cooking
Anne Willan Founder and director of La Varenne Cookery School in Burgundy and West Virginia. Author of many books and a specialist in French cuisine.

Italian Cooking
Anna Del Conte is the author of *The Classic Food of Northern Italy* (chosen as the 1996 Guild of Food Writers Book of the Year) and *The Gastronomy of Italy*. She has appeared on BBC-TV's *Masterchef*.

Vietnamese Cooking

Nicole Routhier One of the United States' most popular cookery writers, her books include *Cooking Under Wraps, Nicole Routhier's Fruit Cookbook* and the award-winning *The Foods of Vietnam.*

Malaysian Cooking

Jill Dupleix One of Australia's best known cookery writers, with columns in the *Sydney Morning Herald* and *Elle*. Author of *New Food, Allegro al dente* and the Master Chefs *Pacific.*

Peking Cuisine

Helen Chen Learned to cook traditional Peking dishes from her mother, Joyce Chen, the grande dame of Chinese cooking in the United States. The author of *Chinese Home Cooking.*

Stir Fries

Kay Fairfax Author of several books, including *100 Great Stir-fries, Homemade* and *The Australian Christmas Book.*

Noodles

Terry Durack Australia's most widely read restaurant critic and co-editor of the *Sydney Morning Herald Good Food Guide*. He is the author of *YUM!*, a book of stories and recipes.

North Indian Curries

Pat Chapman Started the Curry Club in 1982. Appears regularly on television and radio and is the author of eighteen books, the latest being *The Thai Restaurant Cookbook.*

Barbecues and Grills

Brian Turner Chef/patron of Turner's in Knightsbridge and one of Britain's most popular food broadcasters; he appears frequently on *Ready Steady Cook, Food and Drink* and many other television programmes.

Summer and Winter Casseroles

Anton Edelmann Maître Chef des Cuisines at the Savoy Hotel, London, and author of six books. He appears regularly on BBC-TV's *Masterchef.*

Traditional Puddings

Tessa Bramley Chef/patron of the acclaimed Old Vicarage restaurant in Ridgeway, Derbyshire. Author of *The Instinctive Cook*, and a regular presenter on a new Channel 4 daytime series *Here's One I Made Earlier.*

Decorated Cakes

Jane Asher Author of several cookery books and a novel. She has also appeared in her own television series, *Jane Asher's Christmas* (1995).

Favourite Cakes

Mary Berry One of Britain's leading cookery writers, her numerous books include *Mary Berry's Ultimate Cake Book*. She has made many television and radio appearances and is a regular contributor to cookery magazines.

Photographs © Simon Wheeler 1997

First published in 1997 by
George Weidenfeld & Nicolson
The Orion Publishing Group
Orion House
5 Upper St Martin's Lane
London WC2H 9EA

British Library Cataloguing-in-Publication data
A catalogue record for this book is available from
the British Library

ISBN 0 297 82282 9

Designed by Lucy Holmes
Edited by Maggie Ramsay
Food styling by Joy Davies
Typeset by Tiger Typeset